Easy Muffin Tin Meals: Delicious Recipes for Breakfast Lunch and Dinner

Scarlett Aphra

Legal Disclaimer

The information contained herein cannot replace or substitute for the services of trained professionals in any field, including, but not limited to, nutritional matters. Under no circumstances will Echo Bay Books, or any of its representatives or contractors be liable for any damages, including special or consequential damages that result from the use of, or the inability to use, the information, recipes or strategies communicated to these materials or any services provided prior to or following the receipt of these materials, even if advised of the possibility of such damages. Visit your MD before beginning any new diet. You alone are responsible and accountable for your decisions, actions and results in your life, and by your use of these materials, you agree not to attempt to hold us liable for any such decisions, actions or results, at any time, under any circumstance.

Muffin Tin Meals Table of Contents

Part One: All About Muffin Tin Meals

What Are Muffin Tin Meals?

Muffin tin meals are any food that is prepared in a muffin tin instead of a traditional pan, dish, or tray. A muffin tin meal can be breakfast, lunch, dinner, dessert, or a side dish baked straight in a muffin pan.

They're easy, perfect portions that are fun and different to eat. Muffin tin meals are mess-free, too -- there's no cutting of servings required, and they freeze in perfect amounts. Once you start cooking in muffin tins you'll be hooked!

From Concept To Creation: Making Your Own Muffin Tin Meals

Want to try out your own muffin tin meals? We've provided 20 easy recipes for every meal in this book. But if you get eager to try more, you're in luck -- many recipes can be adapted to work in muffin tins. It usually comes down to just spooning the ingredients into a lined or greased muffin tin instead of a baking pan. Once you've become comfortable making these recipes, you'll find it is much easier to adapt your family's favorites into muffin tin portions.

You can already customize many of the meals in this book by leaving out ingredients, like veggies, meats and cheese, or switching them up to suit your tastes. Since every muffin cup is individual, it's easy to leave out ingredients you don't like, and add ones that you do. You can also experiment with half batches to try new meals and experiment with flavors.

There are a few rules and guidelines to follow when baking in muffin tins to get the best results. The main rule is to fill each cup 2/3 full to avoid spilling and burnt tops. Also remember to watch the timer closely – since muffin trays can be different sizes, and oven temperatures can vary, you'll want to keep an eye on your muffin tin meals as the timer nears the end of the bake time.

Aside from that, muffin tin meals are all about having fun and creating easy-to-eat portions, so get in the kitchen and try out some recipes!

Why Muffin Tin Meals?

There are lots of reasons to whip up a batch of muffin tin meals, from their convenience to their novelty. Here are a few of our favorites things about them.

Perfect Portions

Muffin tin meals are fantastic because they come out of the oven already portioned. This helps tremendously with eating a balanced and controlled diet. This makes them ideal for potlucks, picnics, cookouts, and barbecues. There's no slicing, no kids fighting about who gets the biggest piece, and no overeating.

If normal muffin tin portions are too large, you can always use a mini muffin pan instead. Just adjust the cooking time accordingly.

Convenient and Easy

With muffin tin meals, it's easy to scale up or down a recipe because you don't have to recalculate baking time or waste time searching through the cupboards looking for a more suitable pan. Just scoop, bake, and serve!

Kid Friendly

Who doesn't love mini bite-sized version of things? Kids love muffin tin meals because they're different than an ordinary breakfast or dinner. They're a great trick for easy, healthy eating – and they're fun.

For picky eaters, you can easily customize each cup to suit tastes, like leaving out broccoli or meat if someone isn't a fan.

The more you make muffin tin meals, the more you'll discover how easy and convenient they are for busy lifestyles.

Part Two: Muffin Tin Recipes

Breakfast Oat Cups

Makes 10 cups

Ingredients
1 cup oats
9 tablespoons flour
3 tablespoons ground flax
1 teaspoon vanilla
1/4 teaspoon cinnamon
2 tablespoons honey
1/3 cup vegetable oil

Method

Preheat oven to 375F and grease a standard muffin tin.

Mix oats, flour, flax, and cinnamon together in a medium bowl. Add the vanilla, honey, and oil, and stir until well combined into a dough.

Press 1 – 2 tablespoons of the dough into the muffin tins, pressing to form it to the sides. Bake for 10-15 minutes, until lightly golden brown.

Allow to cool before removing.

Nutritional Info
Calories 144
Fat 8.5g
Total Carbohydrates 15.1g
Sugar 3.6g
Protein 2.3g

Pancake Puffs

Yields 18-24 puffs.

Ingredients
1 cup milk
6 eggs
1 cup flour
1/2 teaspoon salt
1 teaspoon vanilla
1/4 cup canola oil

Method

Preheat oven to 400F and grease a standard muffin tin.

Combine all ingredients in a large bowl and whisk until all lumps are gone. Allow to sit for 15-20 minutes.

Scoop the batter into the muffin tins, about 2/3 full. Bake for 10-15 minutes. They'll be puffy and golden brown when ready.

Serve with syrup, fruit, or any other topping of your choice.

Nutritional Info
Calories 60
Fat 3.6g
Total Carbohydrates 4.6g
Sugar 0.6g
Protein 2.3g

Morning Muffins

Yields 12

Ingredients
1 1/2 cups whole wheat flour
1 cup rolled oats
1/2 cup white sugar
1 teaspoon cinnamon
2 teaspoons baking powder
1 teaspoon baking soda
1/2 teaspoon salt
1 egg
3/4 cup milk
1/3 cup vegetable oil
1/2 teaspoon vanilla
1 cup mashed bananas

Method

Preheat oven to 375F, and grease a standard muffin tin.

In a medium bowl, combine the flour, oats, sugar, cinnamon, baking powder, baking soda, and salt. Set aside.

In a large bowl, combine the milk, oil, vanilla, and bananas and mix well. Add to the dry ingredients, and stir until just combined.

Scoop the batter into the muffin tins, about 2/3 to 3/4 full. Bake for 15-20 minutes.

Nutritional Info
Calories 194
Fat 7.3g
Total Carbohydrates 29g
Sugar 10.8g
Protein 3.6g

Mini Quiches

Yields 12-18.

Ingredients

8 eggs
1 tablespoon milk
1/4 cup cheddar cheese, grated
2 cloves garlic, minced
1 red bell pepper, chopped
1 bunch of spinach, chopped
1/4 onion, diced
salt and pepper, to taste

Method

Preheat oven to 350F and grease a standard muffin tin.

In a large bowl, whisk all ingredients together. Scoop the mixture into the muffin tins, about 3/4 full. Bake for 20-30 minutes, until golden brown and cooked through.

Nutritional Info

Calories 42
Fat 2.6g
Total Carbohydrates 1.6g
Sugar 0.6g
Protein 3.5g

Ham and Egg Cups

Yields 2 servings.

Ingredients

2 eggs
2 slices of ham
salt and pepper, to taste
1/4 cup grated cheese (optional)

Method

Preheat oven to 375F.

Place the ham in the muffin tin, molded to the sides like a cup. Crack the egg and place in the ham cup. Sprinkle with salt, pepper and cheese, if desired.

Bake for 15-20 minutes.

Nutritional Info

Calories 109
Fat 6.8g
Total Carbohydrates 1.4g
Protein 10.2g

Hard Boiled Eggs

Yields --

Ingredients
Eggs (this recipe adapts to any amount)
Ice water

Method

Preheat oven to 325F. Place desired amount of eggs
in a muffin tray, and bake for 20 minutes. Remove
and place immediately in the ice water for 10
minutes. Keep refrigerated.

Hashbrown Bites

Yields 12

Ingredients

3 cups russet potatoes, grated and dried (squeeze in a towel)
1/3 cup green onion, chopped
1/2 cup Parmesan cheese, grated
1/2 teaspoon salt
dash of pepper
2 tablespoons vegetable oil

Method

Preheat oven to 350F and grease a standard muffin tray. (You can use a mini muffin tray, too - just check them more frequently as they bake.)

In a large bowl, combine all ingredients and stir well to combine. Scoop the mixture evenly into the muffin tins, and press down slightly to pack the hash browns.

Bake for 45 minutes to an hour, until nicely browned. Cut around the edges and allow to cool before removing.

Nutritional Info

Calories 47
Fat 2.3g
Total Carbohydrates 6.1g
Protein 0.7g

Corn Dog Muffins

Yields 12 – 16.

Ingredients

1/2 cup butter, melted
1 1/2 cups cornmeal
1 cup all purpose flour
3 tablespoons sugar
1 1/2 teaspoons baking powder
1 teaspoon salt
1/2 teaspoon baking soda
1 cup buttermilk
3 large eggs, lightly beaten
1 cup cheddar cheese, grated
2 hot dogs, sliced into 12 pieces

Method

Preheat oven to 400F and grease a standard muffin tray.

In a large bowl, combine the cornmeal, flour, sugar, baking powder, baking soda, and salt. Make a well in the middle and all the butter, buttermilk, and eggs, and mix until just combined. Gently fold in the cheese.

Scoop the batter into the muffin tins, about 2/3 full. Bake for 8 minutes, then press a hot dog piece into the center. Bake for an additional 8-10 minutes, until golden brown. Allow to cool slightly before removing.

Nutritional Info

Calories 261
Fat 15g
Total Carbohydrates 24.6g
Sugar 2.7g
Protein 7.8g

Mac and Cheese Cups

Yields 24

Ingredients

2 cups uncooked macaroni
2 tablespoon butter
1 egg, beaten
1 cup milk
1 1/2 cups sharp cheddar cheese, grated
1/4 cup Parmesan cheese, finely grated
1/4 cup jalapeño Havarti, grated (optional)
1/2 cup Panko bread crumbs
2 teaspoons olive oil
1/2 teaspoon salt
1/4 teaspoon pepper

Method

Preheat oven to 350F and grease a muffin tin.

Cook the macaroni according to package directions, drain, and place back into the pot. While the pasta cooks combine the Panko, oil, and salt and pepper in a small bowl.

Add the butter and egg to the pasta and stir until evenly coated. Add the cheeses, and stir until mostly melted and well combined. Spoon the pasta into the muffin tins and sprinkle the bread crumbs over top.

Bake for 30 minutes. The top will be golden brown and the pasta will be bubbling. Allow to cool slightly before removing from the pan.

Nutritional Info

Calories 92
Fat 5.1g
Total Carbohydrates 7.5g
Sugar 0.9g
Protein 4.1g

Shepherd's Pie

Ingredients
Filling:
1 lbs lean ground beef
1 teaspoon Worchester sauce
1/2 teaspoon salt
1/2 teaspoon freshly ground pepper
1 teaspoon smoked paprika
1 teaspoon cayenne pepper
2 – 3 cloves garlic, minced
2 teaspoons onion powder
1/2 cup peas
1/2 cup corn
2 tablespoons flour
1 cup beef or chicken stock

Potatoes:
1 1/2 - 2 lbs potatoes (3 or 4 large russet potatoes)
2 tablespoons butter
1/4 milk or cream
1/2 cup grated cheese (optional)

Method

Preheat the oven to 350F and line a muffin tin with paper or silicone liners. Peel, wash, and cube each potato and place in a large pot full of cold salted water. Simmer until tender, about 20 to 30 minutes. To prepare the filling, brown the ground beef in a medium skillet with the oil, and season with the garlic, salt, pepper, paprika, onion powder, and cayenne, making sure to cook thoroughly to avoid death.

Drain the liquid from the beef into a measuring cup, then set the meat aside in a bowl while you make the gravy. Whisk in one cup of beef broth mixed with the flour, and stir constantly, making sure all the lumps are out. Once the gravy thickens slightly, add the frozen vegetables, quinoa, and beef, and stir until heated and well combined. Mash the potatoes with the butter and milk, and season to taste. Scoop the beef mixture into the lined muffin tins. Pipe the mashed potatoes on top.

Bake for about 25-30 minutes, until bubbly and brown.

Nutritional Info
Calories 82
Fat 3.0g
Total Carbohydrates 6.5g
Protein 7.2g

Taco Bites

Yields 12

Ingredients

1 pound ground beef cooked with taco seasoning
12 tortillas
1 1/2 cups cheddar cheese, grated
Preferred Toppings

Method

Cut large circles (about 5 inches wide) out of the
tortillas. Shape them to fit the muffin tins. Spoon the
beef evenly into the tortillas, and sprinkle with
cheese.

Bake for 15-20 minutes, until browned and bubbling.
Remove from oven, add your favorite toppings, and
enjoy!

Chicken and Broccoli Cups

Yields 12

Ingredients

2 cups cooked chicken, diced
1 can cream of chicken soup
1 cup broccoli, diced
1 garlic clove, minced
salt and pepper, to taste
Premade biscuit dough
1/4 cup grated Parmesan cheese (optional)

Method

Preheat oven to 375F and grease a standard muffin tin.

Combine the first five ingredients, tossing to mix well. Press the biscuit dough into the muffin tins, contouring to the sides of the pan. Spoon the chicken mixture into the dough cups, and sprinkle with the cheese.

Bake for 20-30 minutes, until golden brown.

Nutritional Info

Calories 79
Fat 3.0g
Total Carbohydrates 4.6g
Protein 8.0g

Corn Bread Muffins

Yields 12 – 16

Ingredients
1/2 cup vegetable oil
1 cup cornmeal
1 1/2 cups all purpose flour
1/4 cup sugar
1 1/2 teaspoons baking powder
1 teaspoon salt
1/2 teaspoon baking soda
1 cup buttermilk
3 large eggs, lightly beaten

Method

Preheat oven to 400F and grease a standard muffin tray.

In a large bowl, combine the cornmeal, flour, sugar, baking powder, baking soda, and salt. Make a well in the middle and all the butter, buttermilk, and eggs, and mix until just combined.

Scoop the batter into the muffin tins, about 2/3 full. Bake for 20-25 minutes, until golden brown and cooked through.

Nutritional Info
Calories 217
Fat 11g
Total Carbohydrates 25.3g
Protein 4.7g

Sweet Potato Gratin

Yields 16-18

Ingredients

2 medium sweet potatoes, thinly sliced
1/4 cup light cream
1/4 cup Parmesan Cheese
salt and pepper, to taste

Method

Preheat oven to 400F, and grease a standard muffin tin.

Place a few slices of the sweet potatoes in each muffin spot, seasoning with a pinch of salt, pepper, and cheese. Keep layering and seasoning the potatoes until the cups are filled about 2/3 full, then pour 1-2 teaspoons of cream over top. Sprinkle the remaining cheese, then bake for 30-35 minutes. They will be golden brown and tender when ready.

Allow to cool for a few minutes and then remove from the pan.

Nutritional Info

Calories 28
Fat 1g
Total Carbohydrates 5.3g
Protein 0.3g

Chocolate Buns

Ingredients
Dough
2 1/4 cups all purpose
2 tbsp sugar
2 1/2 tsp baking power
1/2 tsp baking soda
1/2 tsp salt
1/2 cup cold butter, cubed
1 cup buttermilk

Filling
3 tablespoons butter, room temperature
1/4 cup sugar
1 1/2 cups semisweet chocolate
1/4 cup cocoa powder

Method

Preheat oven to 350F.

In a large bowl, stir together the flour, sugar, baking powder, baking soda, and salt. Using a pastry blender or 2 knifes (or your hands, whatever works), cut in butter until mixture resembles coarse crumbs. Stir in yogurt to make a soft, slightly sticky dough.

Flour your hands, and press the dough into a ball. Knead gently about 10 times. Then roll out the dough to about 35x30cm (14x12in).

Now it's time to make the filling. Combine the butter, sugar, chocolate, and cocoa powder in a blender and pulse until well mixed. Crumble the mixture over the dough, leaving about a 2 cm border. Brush border with water, and roll the dough as if it were a jellyroll.

Using a serrated knife, cut into 14 slices. Place into greased muffin tins, and bake for 15-20 minutes, or until golden brown.

Nutritional Info
Calories 268
Fat 14.8g
Total Carbohydrates 32.6g
Protein 4.3g

Brownie Bites

Yields 24

Ingredients
1 cup butter, melted
1 cup white sugar
1 cup brown sugar
3/4 cup cocoa
3 eggs
1 cup flour
1 1/2 teaspoon baking powder
1 teaspoon vanilla
1 cup semi-sweet chocolate chips

Method

Preheat oven to 350F and grease two mini muffin pans.

In a large bowl, combine the butter, sugars, cocoa, and eggs, and beat until glossy and smooth. Add the flour, baking powder, and vanilla, and mix until well combined.

Pour the batter into the mini muffin pan and sprinkle with chocolate chips. Bake for 7-10 minutes, until a toothpick inserted in the centre comes out clean.

Nutritional Info
Calories 157
Fat 8.6g
Total Carbohydrates 19.9g
Protein 1.8g

Apple Pies

Yields 12

Ingredients
1 package pre-made pie crust
5 apples, peeled and diced
3/4 cup sugar
2 teaspoons cinnamon
6 tablespoons flour
2 tablespoons butter

Method

Preheat oven to 425F, and set aside a muffin pan.

Roll out the pastry dough to about 1/4 inch thick, and cut 12 4-5 inch circles. Press them into the muffin cups, forming to the edges.

In a large bowl, mix the apples, sugar, cinnamon, flour, and butter until well combined. Spoon the mixture into the muffin cups. Bake for for 16-18 minutes, until the crust is golden and the pies are bubbling.

Nutritional Info
Calories 129
Fat 2.5g
Total Carbohydrates 27.3g
Protein 0.5g

Snickerdoodle Blondie Bites

Yields 30 - 36

Ingredients

2 2/3 cups all-purpose flour
2 teaspoons baking powder
1 teaspoon cinnamon
1/4 teaspoon ground nutmeg
1 teaspoon salt
2 cups brown sugar
1 cup butter
2 eggs
1 tablespoon vanilla
2 tablespoons sugar
2 teaspoons cinnamon
1/4 teaspoon nutmeg

Method

Preheat oven to 350F and grease two mini muffin pans.

In a medium bowl, combine the flour, baking powder, cinnamon, nutmeg and salt and set aside. In large bowl, beat together butter and brown sugar until creamy. Add in the eggs and vanilla and beat until glossy. Add the flour mixture, and mix until combined.

In a small bowl, combine the sugar, cinnamon and nutmeg.

Spoon the batter into the mini muffin pans, about 2/3 full, and sprinkle with the spiced sugar mix. Bake for 5-10 minutes, and allow to cool slightly before removing from pan.

Nutritional Info

Calories 118
Fat 5.5g
Total Carbohydrates 16.1g
Protein 1.3g

Hazelnut Cupcakes

Yields 16 cupcakes

Ingredients

1 cup flour
1 teaspoon baking powder
pinch of salt
1/2 cup unsweetened cocoa powder
1/2 cup butter, room temperature
1 cup sugar
1/2 cup Nutella
2 eggs, room temperature
1/2 cup buttermilk
2 teaspoon vanilla

Method

Preheat oven to 350 degrees and grease a muffin pan.

In a medium bowl, whisk the dry ingredients together and set aside. In the bowl of a stand mixer, beat the butter and sugar until creamy. Add the Nutella and eggs and beat until well combined. Combine the milk and vanilla, and add to the batter in alternating batches with the flour. Spoon the batter into the muffin cups until 2/3 full, then bake for 20-25 minutes.

Nutella Frosting

Ingredients

1/2 cup butter, room temperature
1/2 cup nutella
3 cups icing sugar, sifted
1 - 2 tbsp cream (if needed)

Method

In the bowl of a large mixer, whip butter and Nutella until creamy. Gradually add in icing sugar until desired consistency is reached. Add cream if needed.

Nutritional Info

Calories 381
Fat 16.8g
Total Carbohydrates 57.3g
Protein 3.2g

Baked Apples

Yields 6

Instructions
6 apples, cored
2 tablespoons lemon juice
1/4 cup brown sugar
1/4 cup all purpose flour
3 tablespoons butter, chilled
1/4 cup rolled oats
1 teaspoon cinnamon
1/4 teaspoon cloves
1/2 cup walnuts, chopped
1/4 cup raisins

Method

Preheat oven to 350F.

Place each cored apple in a cup in a muffin pan, and
sprinkle with lemon juice so they don't brown.

In a medium bowl, combine the sugar, flour, butter, oats,
cinnamon, cloves, walnuts, and raisins. Toss to mix well.
Spoon the filling into the apples -- you may have to press
it down to fill it well.

Bake for 25-30 minutes, until the apples are tender,
golden, and the filling is bubbling.

Nutritional Info
Calories 285
Fat 12.3g
Total Carbohydrates 43.6g
Protein 3.8g

ONE LAST THING

We would love to get your feedback about our book:

If you enjoyed this book or found it useful, we would be very grateful if you would post a short review on Amazon. Your support really does make a difference and we read all of the reviews personally, so we can get your feedback and make our books even better.

Thank you again for your support!

Sign up for free ebooks

Echo Bay Books is proud to bring you our latest and greatest eBooks on Amazon. We treat you as a guest, and we treat our guests well. We promise to only send you notifications if it has some goodies attached that we think you will like. We launch our eBooks for free for the first 5 days every time. That means you will be the first to know when new books launch (once per week) - for FREE. No spam, ever. Just follow this link http://eepurl.com/zYTDH and sign up!

Manufactured by Amazon.ca
Bolton, ON

26160675R00036